Day Trading

Definitive Beginner's Guide

Table Of Contents

Introduction

Wall Street, the New York Stock Exchange, stocks, bonds, mutual funds. These names and products are a fundamental part of this country's financial history. For most of the United State's history, high finance was the domain of investment professionals, mainly employed by established financial houses. Perhaps the most stereotypical image the average American has of the "market" dates back to the days of the "Roaring 20's," the great stock market crash, and the great depression. Investment trading has changed a great deal since then. One of the biggest changes is how the investment world has opened up in many ways to the small investor. Whereas once, the small investor had to go through a broker, and make a fairly large committment in funds (at least to them), in order to "get in the game." Over time, the restrictions on small investors have been loosened, in part a reflection of their greater education (many people have college educations today, while in the pre-depression stock market days, the average person often wasn't even a high school graduate), and in part because many more small investors are smarter when it comes to investments too (mainly because they have access to books and materials such as this one). Over time, small investors gained access to a variety of mutual funds, blended funds (a mutual fund that invests in several other funds to create a more diversified portfolio), lifestyle funds (geared to meeting the needs of investors at different stages of their lives), and then, discount investment brokers who were geared toward small investors and their smaller share purchases.

Of course all of these innovations still keep the small investor at least an arms length from the actual trading of stocks. It wasn't until regulations loosened enough to permit small investors to make their own investments via their own computers. This led to some small investors whose goal was to maximize their profits by "playing" the market. These adventurous investors looked to make short term investments (buying and selling the same stock in less than a day) to take advantage of the small swings in share prices that happen with many stocks. "Day trading" is a product of the computer/internet age. Thanks to a variety of technological and regulatory innovations, it has become possible for anyone with investment capital and access to the internet to make money as an investor by taking advantage of those tiny swings in prices throughout the course of the day. It's incredibly important to keep in mind though, just as a small investor can make a lot of money in investment markets, they can also lose a lot. Day traders don't get any guarantees, and more than a few have lost everything by playing the market poorly. This book will try to give the small investor the knowledge and tools to have a fighting chance of making money through day trading.

For the successful day trader, investment intelligence can lead to freedom from the workplace and provide a source of passive income, money that comes in with minimal effort by the investor. There's nothing like getting paid for doing almost nothing!

Chapter 1:
Money Makes the World Go Round

"Risk comes from not knowing what you're doing." – Warren Buffet

The investment world may seem daunting and complicated to you, the new investor, particularly since you're playing for "real" money – your money. As a novice to the world of investment and money management, you need to learn the basics and even the language of the investment world. While not as difficult as say learning ancient Latin, the language of investment can be bewildering to you. That's okay. You're going to learn all about investing in financial markets in this e-book, beginning with this chapter.

You may look at a system such as the "stock market" and think it's a form of legalized gambling. Unlike the gaming in places like Monaco, Las Vegas, and Atlantic City though, there is an important fundamental difference between market investment and casino gambling. When you're putting your money down in a casino, you're not buying anything except a chance to increase your stake. When you put your money into a stock, bond, or other investment vehicle, you're either buying a small part of a company (a "share" or multiple "shares" of the company) or loaning that company or municipality, or government money. "Losing" at a casino means your entire bet is gone. "Losing" in the investment market on the other hand means your investment has lost some value, but not necessarily all of it. In fact, depending on the nature of your investment in the market, the value of an investment can drop and you can still make money through techniques known as "selling short" and buying "puts" and "calls." (Here are examples of the language and vocabulary you were warned about earlier. In each chapter of this book you'll learn about the concepts and techniques these terms represent and how you can use them to make money. First, you should learn about how investments work.

Stocks

Imagine a small business that is in the process of growing. Perhaps it's an innovative sandwich maker. The business is a winner, barely able to keep up with demand, so the owner decides to open a second store, and then a third. They're all so successful that people are asking if they can get a piece of the action. Now the owner is selling "franchises" to other investors. As this small business transitions into a bigger business, it finds it needs things it didn't when it was a single shop. It needs a headquarters, a supply chain, marketing, legal team, and many other things. It also needs money to be able to get and maintain these things. As the business owner, you have several ways of raising this money. You can go to your local bank (or a much bigger bank) and borrow some money via a loan. We'll talk more about loans as investment a little later in this chapter, since even the novice individual investor can play the loan market too. Let's say though, that in this example, the business owner doesn't want to go the loan route.

Maybe the bank wants to charge too much for the use of its money (interest and fees), or maybe the bank considers the risks of the loan aren't worth it (risk/reward is a very important concept when it comes to your investments, something we'll get to later). Because of that, he wants to try a different way of getting funding.

In this case, our business owner decides he's willing to sell off part of the business to raise money to reinvest in the business (or to take some money out of the business as a reward for his hard work). He does this by issuing "shares" of stock in the business. Based on the business's "valuation," its worth in terms of total assets minus total liabilities, the initial share price will be a reflection of that value along with the potential that business has to offer. That last part is important to understand. The value of a stock or loan to an investor has a lot to do with the potential value of that investment based on the market's understanding of that value. In our example, the business owner (through intermediaries who actually manage the process) divides the value of the business into these small increments (shares), sets an initial value, based on the valuation of the company, then offers those shares through a market where investors can buy and sell those shares. As an investor, you may not be able to afford one of the franchises this business offers, but you can afford to buy or sell shares of ownership. While it may costs tens of thousands of dollars to invest in a franchise, individual stocks can sell for as little as a few cents. "Penny" stocks, as they're known, offer a really cheap way for an investor to buy into a company, but also tend to be very high risk as well. Let's take a look at the basics of stock investment:

- Stock shares

- Dividends

- Stock market

- Broker

- Commissions

- Trades

Stock Shares

There are two types of stock, "preferred" stock, and "common" stock. Preferred stock is in some ways more typical of a loan investment than a stock investment. Preferred stock prices usually don't "move" (change prices up or down) very much compared to common stock prices. They do offer several benefits over common stock though. For one thing, they're usually guaranteed a fixed income (interest return, aka a "dividend") for as long as the investor holds the stock (one way the stock is closer to a loan investment). The other advantage a share of preferred stock offers is that if the company is liquidated (broken down into component parts and sold off), the preferred stock holder has a higher chance of getting some money back, once higher priority investors are paid off. Preferred stock shareholders rarely get a vote during shareholder decision-making. The company has the option of "calling" these shares, in other words, buying the shares back, usually at a premium.

"Common" stock on the other hand usually offers voting rights since the shareholder is considered an "owner" of the company. Unlike the price of preferred shares, which are generally pretty stable, the price of common stock shares can be from slightly to incredibly volatile. In plain English, the price of a share of preferred stock may not go up or down more than a few cents from year to year, while the price of a share of common stock may go up or down significantly over the course of a few days (or sometimes much, much, faster). While this volatility may be the stuff of ulcers for some investors, it's where you can make money – a lot of money – can be made and lost, particularly for the day trader. Your goal is not to invest for the long haul, but to take advantage of these shifts that take place over the course of a single day.

Dividends

There's another way an investor can make money off of a share of common stock, through the distribution of dividends. Unlike preferred shares though, dividends for common stock are not guaranteed. Instead they are issued at the discretion of the company. Some companies offer predictable, regular dividends (usually in industries and companies that have been around a while and are pretty much done with rapid growth). Other companies may rarely, or even, never pay a dividend. You see, dividends don't just cost a company money, they can also cost a company opportunity. Most young and growing companies prefer to take profits and use them to continue expanding, making the business more profitable. Generally, the price of a share of stock declines based on the value of a dividend, simply because the company is worth less after paying shareholders. It's useful for a trader to be aware of a company's history of dividend payments simply because it can be an indicator of how the company is doing. For instance, if a firm has a history of paying a dividend ever quarter and suddenly stops or drastically reduces its dividend, it can indicate either a decline in the business (or an entire industry), or hint at the company needing to build up cash reserves for some reason (expansion, fighting off an attempt from another concern trying to take over the company, changes in regulations governing how that company does business, or other issues).

Broker (Stock Broker)

While there are a few exceptions (involving a couple of investment techniques that are the opposite of day trading), companies do not usually sell shares of stock to individuals. Instead, a middleman known as a "stock broker" will handle the buying and selling of shares for an investor. At one time, your choices as a small investor were pretty limited in this regard. Generally stockbrokers were not interested in small fry like you, or charged enough "commission" (their fee for handling the transaction) that it often wasn't worthwhile for the small investor. The past few decades have greatly changed the buyer/broker dynamic though. Through the advent of discount brokers (such as Charles Schwab) and online brokers (such as E-trade), the small trader has easier, faster, and cheaper access to the investment market. Easier, faster, and cheaper are vitally important concepts for the day trader to master.

Commissions

Commissions are the price you pay to buy and sell stocks. This is no small issue for the day trader since the money you spend paying commissions is an expense you have to pay whether you make money or not. The cost of commissions can also reduce your profit or extend your loss if not carefully contained. You have a number of options when it comes to finding a brokerage (company of brokers) to handle your trades. These are often big name firms you'll see advertising on TV such as Fidelity Brokerage, TD Ameritrade, TradeKing, and Scott Trade to name a few. It's not unusual for them to offer introductory offers that include free trades and other incentives to new trades, so shop carefully when you're looking for a brokerage account.

Trades

When you buy or sell a share of stock, you're engaged in a "trade." As a novice trader, it's important that you remember there are two sides to a trade, and no, they don't have to be completed in a specific order. With stocks, you can actually sell a stock you don't own – something known as "short selling," and then later buy the stock. This process involves borrowing the shares you're selling from someone else, and hoping the price of that stock goes down before you have to return your borrowed shares. You should also remember, it's not enough to buy a stock at a good time; you also have to manage to sell it at a good time. There are some basic investment techniques you need to be aware of:

- Short Selling

- Leverage

- Arbitrage

- Bid/Ask Price and Spread

- Market Timing

Short Selling

As you just read, short selling involves the borrowing of a share(s) from one investor, selling it, then buying enough shares of the same stock to replace the ones you borrowed at a later time, and hopefully after the price of those shares has gone down. Short selling has been a bit controversial in the past. Many investors blamed the 1929 stock market crash on short sellers driving down share prices. Others argued that short selling actually guaranteed a market for stocks since the short sellers had to eventually buy shares to end their position in those stocks. For a while, regulators maintained an "uptick" rule, requiring investors to wait until a stock showed an increase (no matter small) in price, before being able to begin a short sale. That requirement was removed a few years ago.

Here's an example of how a short sale transaction works:

You borrow 100 shares of XYZ corporation, which are currently selling for $10 a share. You're now on the hook for $10,000 worth of stock, plus the money you have to pay the shareholder for the loan of their stock. This is usually expressed as an interest rate (around 4% or so at the time this book was written) per month. The amount of interest paid is calculated by the formula Market Value x Interest Rate x number of days divided by 360.

You sell the shares you've borrowed while the shares are selling for $10, and three days later, buy your replacement shares at a time when they were selling for $9 a share. You've realized a gain of $1,000 from this maneuver, but you still have to pay for trading commissions and for the loan of the shares. Let's say your discount broker charges a fixed rate of $5.00 per trade (a very good rate at this time), and you're paying this fee every time you buy and sell (meaning the full transaction costs you $10). Using our formula above we also have to calculate the interest owed on the borrowed shares. This is calculated on the market rate of the shares when you borrowed them. So our calculation looks like this: 100 shares x $10/per share = $10,000 x 4% = $400 x 3/360 = 3.33. After making good on the borrowed shares, your profit on the maneuver is $1,000 − $10 - $3.33 = $890.67. Keep in mind though, in a simple stock transaction, when you buy a stock, the worst you can do is lose the value of your investment. When shorting a stock, you can lose more (a lot more) than the value of your investment.

Go back to our example. Suppose the stock you borrowed goes up in price instead of down, and you have to buy back shares for $300 a share. Now, instead of $1,000 profit, you've realized a $20,000 loss, plus you still have to pay the $10 commission and $.33 interest fee. Your initial plan to risk $10,000 has resulted in a loss of $20,010.33. This is why it's important to really know what you're doing when planning a short sale.

Leverage

If you looked at the $890.67 return in the example above, and wondered if there was a way to juice up your returns, then understanding how to use leverage to bolster your returns will help. Just understand, leverage too works both ways. It can magnify your gains and losses.

Lets take that $10,000 you started with. Your broker may allow you to open what's known as a "margin account." Now, you can buy a stock, without paying for it completely. This is a separate account from your "cash" account, which is the account you would normally buy stocks from. It's not unusual for a brokerage to allow a 50% margin. This means the investor puts up half the cost of the stock purchase, and the broker loans the buyer enough to cover the other 50%. As you would expect, the broker will charge you interest for the use of its money. Keep in mind, the longer you borrow the money, the more interest you'll pay, and if that accrued interest accumulates, you may face higher interest rates as a result. Buying "on margin" works really well when you buy low and sell high. Since you were able to buy $15,000 worth of stock while only putting up $1,000 of your own money, you get all the increased value (minus trading commission and interest) of the investment and not just the increased value of your $10,000. The reverse all occurs, if the stock goes down in value. Let's look at both scenarios.

You put $10,000 on the line and your broker buys you $15,000 worth of XYZ stock. A week later, you sell the stock for $20,000. While this would be described as a $5,000 gain in value ($20,000 - $15,000), but from your perspective, it's actually a $10,000 gain, since only $10,000 of your money was involved. You still have to pay your trade commission ($5) and the interest on your margin loan. Let's say your margin fee is 5%. You'll end up paying 5% of the amount borrowed multiplied by the number of days you've kept the shares multiplied by three divided by 360. In our example, this would be $5,000 x 5% x 7 (days)/360 = $250 x .0195 = $4.95 plus the $5 commission. Your profit ends up being $10,000 – $9.95 or $9,991.05. That's a pretty nice return on your initial $10,000 investment!

Your increased investment power has magnified your gain significantly. Unfortunately, the reverse can also happen. Buying on margin can generate losses than can be greater than your initial investment. Margin purchases face other potential problems as well. For a start, the federal government regulates how much margin a brokerage can provide and an investor can use. While it's 50% at the time of this writing, it can change. If you're holding stocks on margin and the fed reduces the maximum margin rate, you'll have to come up with enough money to make up the difference. In our example, lets say the fed lowers the margin maximum to 40%, then you're only allowed to borrow $4,000 on margin, instead of the $5,000 you and your brokerage originally agreed to. You're now subject to a "margin call." In other words, your broker may contact you and request additional money to make up the deficit. Another event can also trigger a margin call; the value of your stocks goes down. Your broker will have a "maintenance margin" requirement. It varies, for our examples, lets use 50% of the value of the original position is a reasonable point for this book.

You've invested $10,000 of your own money in the stock, plus $5,000 on margin when the company's shares were selling at $100 per share, ending up with 150 shares of stock. A week later, the price of the individual shares has fallen to $50 a share, triggering a margin call. Since your 150 shares of stock are now only worth $7,500, the equity in your margin account has dropped from $10,000 to $2,500 ($7,500 stock value - $5,000 equity in margin account after margin loan is subtracted). Since 50% of $15,000 is $7,500, your broker is probably going to ask you for another $5,000 to bring your account back above the maintenance margin. You may have noticed my use of qualifying words ("may," "probably"). This is because your broker is not required to ask you for more money, he has the option of selling as much of your stock holding as needed to bring your position back in line with requirements. He's not even required to tell you he's doing this.

Arbitrage

Sometimes, a trader can take advantage of the inequities of the various financial markets. Suppose you can borrow $100,000 at 5% interest from a bank here in the United States and then loan that money for 10% interest in another country's bank? You would be able to make 5% interest on money that isn't even yours. You are assuming some risk though. The bank you're loaning the money too, may not be as stable as the banks here in the United States. If it defaults on your loan, you're on the hook for that money.

Another approach is to take advantage of the inefficiency of financial markets. Suppose you buy stock in a Japanese company on the Tokyo stock exchange that's selling for $10 a share, knowing that the same stock was listed on the New York Stock Exchange for $15 a share. You'd be able to sell your shares for a profit of $5 per share minus commission simply because the New York Stock Exchange wasn't up to date on the value of the Japanese company. (This is kind of an extreme example. Major stock exchanges work very hard to prevent this kind of thing from happening.) Still, arbitrage opportunities do occur. If you pursue one, be careful to calculate the transaction costs carefully. If they are greater than your arbitrage advantage, you'll lose money.

Bid/Ask Price

Buying stocks isn't quite like going into the grocery story and buying a bag of flour. As I mentioned early, it's just as important for you to consider the selling end of the transaction, as it is the buying end. You'll have to deal with two different prices when making stock transactions. When buying, you'll be dealing with the "Ask price." This is the price the stock owner is willing to sell the stock shares for. If you are selling the stock, then you'll be offered the "Bid price," or the price the buyer is willing to pay for the shares. The difference between these two is known as the "spread." The size of the spread is often used as an indicator of the liquidity of the stock. Small spreads indicate a strong market for the stock; large ones indicate a weak one.

Let's consider a stock with a bid/ask pricing of $20.00/$20.10. This means a buyer would have to pay $20.10 a share, while a sell could expect to get $20.00 per share for the stock he is selling. The spread ($.10) is the fee the "market maker" collects for the transaction. Market makers are dealers or brokers who "make" a market in a particular stock by holding quantities of that stock for sale or purchase with individual buyers.

Market Timing

"Buy low and sell high," is the mantra of most investors. Some, believe in predicting the market so well that they can maximize their returns by buying and selling at optimum points. Market timing is very difficult to do well. Missing by just a small amount of time can result in losses instead of profits. Still, understanding market timing and take advantage of it, are part of being a successful day trader. Instead of trying to time the peaks and valleys of the market though, the day trader is merely trying to understand the market well enough to spot and benefit from movements in stock prices rather than trying to time an overall market.

Chapter 2:
Understanding the Financial Markets

"In this business if you're good, you're right six times out of ten. You're never going to be right nine times out of ten." – Peter Lynch

The investment market isn't just one entity. There are actually multiple "markets" you can participate in as a day trader, both here in the United States, and overseas. This chapter will help you understand these markets and help you chose which ones you want to participate in. In this chapter, you are going to learn about markets for stocks and other entities that represent "things." Keep in mind, the actual trading takes place via a market exchange, such as the New York Stock Exchange:

- Equities (the "stock market")

- Spot Market (also known as the "Cash Market)

- Futures Market

- Derivatives Market

Equities Market

This is the "stock" market. As you read earlier, stocks are shares of a company. These shares can be owned by individual investors, investment brokerages, mutual funds, and of course, the companies themselves. In fact, companies often buy back their own stock (this is a potential opportunity for a day trader by the way). The term "stock market" can refer to a market of American stocks, or Japanese stocks, or Asian stocks, etc.

Stocks are usually traded on stock "exchanges," such as the New York Stock Exchange or the NASDAQ. Generally, stock exchanges handle stocks from a particular region or country. In England, the London Stock Exchange Group handles the British equities market, while the Hong Kong Stock Exchange handles the stocks of Hong Kong based companies. There are about 20 stock exchanges worldwide. As a novice day trader, you need to understand the market you plan on trading in and the particular segment of that market that you are trading in. As you gain experience, you can consider branching out your investments into more than one market, remembering that lack of knowledge in any one market can be costly. While trading in the stock market is what most people automatically think of for day trading, that doesn't have to be true. Remember, as a day trader, you're trying to make money on the little movements of money during the course of the day. While it can be the money movements found in stock prices, there are other markets whose instruments prices also fluctuate.

Spot Market

This market specializes in immediate results rather than future ones, although it can include futures trades that are less than a month from closing. This market is more a tool of big organizations that need to purchase large amounts of commodities or financial instruments immediately.

Futures Market

You may have heard of the futures market. It's often used in movies as a vehicle for the protagonist to make or lose a fortune in a matter of hours. The movie "Trading Places," (Dan Akroyd, Eddie Murphy), being an example. There are a couple of reasons why the futures market makes this possible. First, you're dealing with large amounts of things, and second, you're dealing with leverage – a lot of leverage.

"Futures" are contracts, which allow you to buy or sell something at a set price a set amount of time in the future. This is a pretty useful feature for a big cereal maker, for instance, who can lock up a large quantity of wheat or grain a year or so ahead of time. By buying a series of contracts over a staggered period of time, the cereal maker smoothes out price fluctuations over time. Another advantage is the manufacturer can structure purchases to reflect anticipated demand over time. Since there is a vibrant futures market, the manufacturer can even get out of these contracts by selling some of them if their sales decline.

While futures are a very useful tool for big organizations that need to plan far in advance, they can also be very powerful (and dangerous) investment vehicles for the small investor.

Since they involve selling the right to buy or sell a commodity at a certain date, these contracts can fluctuate greatly in value.

Suppose a big agribusiness expects to produce a certain sized crop this fall. Rather than wait until the fall to try to sell the crop, it will offer a future contract for the delivery of a certain amount of the crop at the current price per bushel or pound or whatever increment that crop is usually measured in. Since this is big business, it also means a lot of that particular item. A buyer then comes along and purchases the contract. This buyer may represent that big cereal company locking up supplies for the future, or, an investor of modest means speculating on the market for that commodity.

What happens if the price of that particular crop drops the next day? Well, if you're the one who just bought the contract committing you to buy the crop at a higher price, you just lost some money. Since futures contracts control huge amounts of a product and offer large amounts of leverage. Depending on the commodity, the leverage involved can range from as much as 10 times the contract's value to hundreds of times its value or more. This means a small investor can take on enormous risk and make or lose a lot of money in very little time.

While you might find this very tempting, keep in mind, you'll be competing against buyers for big corporations. These are people whose job it is to keep track of and predict price movements for their particular supply needs. They will have access to better information than you and also to better models and resources than you. If you are interested in trading in futures contracts you should plan on being well funded, be willing to take on big risks, and have a strong stomach. You should also plan on learning a lot about the commodity you want to trade in. Futures markets are dangerous investments for novice traders.

Derivatives Market

You may remember the word "derivatives" from the financial meltdown almost a decade ago. These instruments are "derived" from other financial products such as mortgages and other loans. An organization will bundle a large group of such loans, and then sell products derived (or created) from those bundles. They fall into two different categories; exchange controlled and over the counter. Exchanges that trade derivatives are regulated. Over the counter derivatives trades are not.

Derivatives, like futures contracts, do serve an important purpose; they give investors a way of "hedging" their bets. This means you can lessen risks through the use of the appropriate derivative. There are plenty of investors who trade in derivatives in a speculative manner. These investors are taking on risk rather than trying to diminish risk like hedgers.

Chapter 3:
Money Related Financial Markets

Investors don't just put money in tangible goods; they also put money into "money" in the form of cash investment products. These markets include:

- Capital Market (handles both stocks and bonds)

- Bond Market (bonds are debt instruments similar to loans)

- Money Market

Capital Markets

"Capital" refers to the money businesses and economies need to operate. A company or individual can be very wealthy, yet still be very "cash poor." In other words, the company many hold valuable assets, but those assets are difficult to quickly turn into cash. Some examples include land, buildings, factories, mines, operating rights, and patent rights for a few examples. These are known as "illiquid" assets. "Liquid" assets on the other hand, include money in company checking accounts, and investment accounts, bank funds from lines of credit, and any actual cash the company has on hand. Businesses try to manage their liquid assets carefully. If they're holding too much capital in liquid form, their money is working for them. If they're not holding enough, they can end up defaulting on loans or not being able to pay suppliers or workers. Growing businesses, as you read earlier, also frequently need capital to continue their expansion. While an individual who wants to raise cash most likely would go to a bank or finance company, businesses have more options for raising capital. It's the capital markets that provide these options.

Generally, the term "capital" markets refers to ways business can raise money either through the sale of equities (stocks through initial public offerings) or financial instruments such as bonds. One important difference between capital markets and "money" markets is the time frame of the transactions. money markets work with instruments of a year's duration or less, while capital markets are concerned with longer-term instruments. Another difference is that money markets work things such as U.S. Treasury instruments, deposits, and loans; while capital markets deal with equities (stocks) and debt securities (bonds and debentures).

Bond Market

Bonds and debentures are forms of debt securities. One way a business can raise cash is by issuing a debt security. This is basically a loan from an investor rather than a bank. If company assets back this debt, it's called a "bond," if not, it's known as a "debenture." Obviously, debentures are riskier than bonds, since there is no specific asset backing them. These instruments are usually medium to long-term investments. The company will offer them at a discount rate it feels is competitive enough to attract investors, while being as favorable for the company as possible. Some factors that can influence the interest rate on the bond include its length to maturity, the financial rating of the company issuing the bond, and whether or not company assets back the bond.

There are ratings companies such as Standard & Poors, Moody's, and Fitch, which rate the safety of bond offerings.

The higher the rating, the safer the bond is considered (if the company files for bankruptcy, bond holders have a higher priority on its assets than stock holders, but there's still a good chance they won't get all their money back). Bonds fall into several different categories based on their ratings. Generally, an AAA or Aaa (different ratings companies use slightly different designations) is the highest rated bond. These are known as "investment" grade bonds. U.S. Treasure bonds backed by the full faith and credit of the United States government are an example of an investment grade bond. Generally, a bond needs to have a rating no lower than BBB- (or Baa3).

Bonds with rankings of BB+ to D (Baa1 to C) are commonly referred to as "Junk" bonds. Junk bonds will offer higher interest rates than investment grade bonds, since they are riskier investments. There's no sense for an investor to purchase a junk bond offering 3% interest if they can get a treasury bond paying the same rate.

As a day trader though, it isn't the bond interest rate or maturity that you'll care about. It's the money movements these things can affect. Bond can be bought when issued, and then sold by the original buyer, bought by someone else, then resold again. The question the buyer and seller share in the course of this transaction is "What is the bond worth?" Suppose the original bond was a $10,000, 10-year long-term investment that paid 6% interest. It's now two years later, and the bondholder wants to raise some cash. While the bond will pay back the original $10,000 when it reaches maturity, the buyer and seller must also consider how much interest that money will earn during the remaining eight years. The value of the bond can fluctuate greatly over the course of its life. Several things can affect the value of a bond. Let's take a look:

- Interest rate differences – Since it's possible to calculate the value of a bond over its life including interest distributions; it's also possible to compare two bonds value to decide which might be a better investment. In other words, if an investor has a choice between two $10,000, 10-year AAA rated bonds, each with eight years remaining to maturity and one pays 6% interest annually, while the other pays 5% annually, obviously, the first bond is the better value. If the owner of the second bond wants to sell his bond, then he needs to increase the value of his bond's sale somehow. This is done by "discounting" the bond value. The seller of the second bond will ask a lower amount for the price of his bond to make up for the lower interest rate. Discounted bonds are priced to account for this.

- Interest changes – in this instance, the value of a bond fluctuates as interest rates change. If you have a $10,000 bond paying 6% interest annually, with 8 years left of its 10-year maturity and interest rates rise higher than 6%, the value of your bond declines. On the other hand, if interest rates drop below 6%, your bond becomes more valuable.

- Company's financial rating – suppose you hold a AAA rated bond and all of a sudden, the company's credit rating drops to AA? The value of your bond decreases on the secondary market because it is not as safe an investment. The opposite is also true. If the company's credit rating improves, the value of your bond increases on the secondary market.

- Remaining time to maturity – the closer the time to the bond's maturity expiring, the lower the secondary market value will be since the bond won't be earning interest for very long.

- Market/investor confidence – the bond market undergoes swings in confidence just as the stock market does. During times of rising interest rates, bonds lose value, because bonds with lower rates and now worth less. If interest rates decline, then existing bonds paying higher rates are more valuable. This effect can be more pronounced if investors believe the interest rise or decline is part of an ongoing trend rather than a one-time aberration. It is this "speculation" that provides opportunities for the day trader.

The bond market offers the day trader some interesting opportunities. It generally (but not always) runs counter to the direction the stock market is moving. This is because investors tend to pursue better investments. If the stock market is rising, they invest more in stocks. If it is declining, then bonds and their greater safety, become more attractive, providing interest rates are reasonably stable.

Money Market

This market only deals with cash instruments with maturities of a year or less, since these investments are far less volatile than long-term bonds. During their short lifespan, they will experience fewer and smaller interest rate movements, the likelihood of originator default or downgrading is less, and, when investors stagger their purchases over a period of time, provide much greater protection from interest rate swings.

The money market is made up of "safe" investments. Typical examples of money market securities include short-term U.S.

Treasury instruments, and highest rate municipal offerings and corporate "paper" (unsecured promissory notes of less than 270 days duration from highly rated companies).

Money market investments are usually purchased directly from the originator and usually offer much higher entry costs than other markets (i.e. your initial investment will have to be much larger than other investments because these securities are sold in much larger increments).

Money Market mutual funds provide access to this market for the small investor. They are useful places to park cash for the short term. Their interest rates tend to be low, so they're not good long term buys.

Chapter 4:
Day Trading Basics

"Look at market fluctuations as your friend rather than your enemy; profit from folly rather than participate in it." – *Warren Buffet*

It's time for you to take a look at the day trading process works. You could just blindly jump in, but that's a recipe for disaster. Instead, let's get you started on how to smartly engage in day trading.

The first question to ask yourself is how big an investment are you planning on making in your day trading efforts? You need to consider not only how much money you're willing to invest, but also how much time. Many investors look at day trading as an escape from their normal jobs, others see it as an answer to the uncertainties of the job market. While you may hunger to day trade full time, people do succeed as part time day traders while working a primary job. Beginners may also want to spend some time simulating investments to get a feel for how comfortable you are with the process and how much talent you may have. As mentioned in the last paragraph, simply jumping in is not a good idea. You need to understand the investment market, learn to look for indicators that give you an idea of stock movements, and make the most of your opportunities.

Infrastructure Concerns

While it may sound mundane, spending some time on your workspace and technology can be well worth it. Day trading can definitely be stressful, so a work area that provides quiet and privacy can be helpful. Don't underestimate the importance of a reliable Internet connection and a backup method of controlling your investments in case your network goes down. These days it's not hard to have a fast land based Internet connection while also having the ability to use your smartphone as a wireless hotspot if your main connection goes down. It only takes one network failure when you have a big investment on the line, to convince you of the importance of a backup Internet access plan.

Understanding the Market

It's one thing to say you want to invest in stocks. It's another thing to figure out what stocks you should be investing in. Investors break down the market into different sectors such as "retailers," "manufacturers," "utilities," "airlines," "energy," "health care," and others. Day traders can choose to target all these sectors or choose to specialize in one or more. As a beginner, focusing on one sector may be advantageous, particularly if it's one you're already familiar with.

Since as a day trader, you're interested in identifying opportunities for small, changes in stocks, not long-term growth. This means you'll need ample funding. U.S. based day traders need a minimum of $25,000 for their trading account, according to Securities and Exchange Commission (SEC) rules. This means you'd really need at least $30,000 to have some flexibility. Keep in mind; in the U.S. you can currently leverage your trading capital up to 400%. This means that you could control $120,000 worth of stock with your $30,000. As you learned earlier, this also means you could suffer four times the losses on your investments. Be aware too, that if you don't maintain your maintenance margin amount, you can receive a margin call. In planning for your trading account, it would be better to have more funds available, since that would make more stocks available for your consideration. Remember too, it's usually more cost efficient to buy shares in multiples of 100, meaning a small investment kitty will either limit you to cheaply priced stocks or buying stocks in smaller increments than are less cost effective. If you can devote more funds to your trading account, you'll be able to pursue more opportunities, and have the wherewithal to recover from losses.

Calculating a Simple Moving Average

The moving average is a basic tool investors use to monitor a stock's behavior over a defined period of time. The investor simply adds the stock's closing price for a specific period of time (two weeks, a month, a quarter, etc.) and then divides that number by the number of trading days in that period. A trader will calculate a short term moving average and a long term moving average for a stock (actually, you'll probably calculate a few more than this to get a better sense of the stock's behavior). A simple moving average can tell you whether a stock is on a rising or declining trend.

An important point for many traders is when the short term moving average rises above or below the long term moving average. A short term moving average that crosses above a long term moving average often indicates the stock is about to begin an upward trend. The opposite is also true.

One approach to using moving averages compares a specific short term moving average (50 days) with a specific long term moving average (200 days). If the 50 day average moves below the 200 day average, you have a bearish signal. This is known as a "Death Cross." If the 50 average moves above the 200 day average, it is a bullish signal, and is known as a "Golden

Cross." While it would be nice if you could rely solely on such a simple system, remember that relying only on a moving average approach is unreliable. It's better to use this information as another bit of information when making your trading plans.

Choosing a Broker

Once you've decided on your trading allocation, you need to choose a broker or brokerage. There are a number of online discount brokers available to the novice investor. Many will offer you their own electronic trading program. Don't be surprised to get offers for free trades and a bonus for picking their firm. Free trades and cash bonuses are nice, but make sure you choose a broker you feel comfortable with and one that checks out with your research.

The biggest online brokerages include: TD Ameritrade, Scott Trade, Fidelity Brokerage, Charles Schwab, Options Express, Merrill Edge, Robinhood, Loyal3, Options House, EOption, and others. Some like Robinhood offer free trades, making their overhead on charging interest on margin accounts and using customer cash to earn interest. Others may offer more services or access to more investment exchanges. One thing you won't get from any of these discount brokerages though is personal advice. That's the purview of the traditional broker.

In choosing a brokerage, consider the cost of trades, your comfort level with its trading program, and your ability to access the company's website. Also, look into what others are saying about the brokerage and whether or not it handles the investment vehicles you're interested in trading.

Calculating a Simple Moving Average

By following the moving average of a stock, you can get a sense of the stock's behavior. The moving average is a basic tool investors use to monitor a stock's behavior over a defined period of time. The investor simply adds the stock's closing price for a specific period of time (two weeks, a month, a quarter, etc.) and then divides that number by the number of trading days in that period. A trader will calculate a short term moving average and a long term moving average for a stock (actually, you'll probably calculate a few more than this to get a better sense of the stock's behavior). A simple moving average can tell you whether a stock is on a rising or declining trend.

An important point for many traders is when the short term moving average rises above or below the long term moving average. A short term moving average that crosses above a long term moving average often indicates the stock is about to begin an upward trend. The opposite is also true.

One approach to using moving averages compares a specific short term moving average (50 days) with a specific long term moving average (200 days). If the 50 day average moves below the 200 day average, you have a bearish signal. This is known as a "Death Cross." If the 50 average moves above the 200 day average, it is a bullish signal, and is known as a "Golden Cross." While it would be nice if you could rely solely on such a simple system, remember that relying only on a moving average approach is unreliable. It's better to use this information as another bit of information when making your trading plans rather than making it the basis of your investment strategy.

Buy Orders, Sell Orders, and Setting a Stop Loss Price

Not every move a trader makes has to be executed immediately or at random. You can tell your brokerage you only want to buy or sell a stock when it hits a certain price. The risk of course, is that the stock may not hit that price while you have money planned for it.

You should also plan on setting a "Stop loss price," too. This is a protective move to make sure you don't get badly burned by the stock price moving in the wrong direction. Let's say you've bought shares of XYZ Corporation when their price was at $4.50 a share. Based on your research, you expect an upward move by the share price and plan on selling when it reaches $4.75 a share (always have an exit price planned). Then something goes wrong. Bad news upsets the market (in general or it effects your stock in particular), and your stock price starts dropping instead. Wisely, you left a stop loss order with your broker, in effect instructing the broker to automatically sell your shares when their price drops to a certain point (perhaps in this example $4.35) to limit your loss. You should know that stop loss orders aren't foolproof. Your broker still has to find someone to buy the shares at that point. In times of crisis, share prices can fall so fast that they blow by the stop loss price and keep going before they finally sell, making your loss bigger than anticipated. While this isn't a regular occurrence, unexpected events can cause them. The company selling the Epi-pen recently saw it's valuation drop $3 billion dollars in a short period of time because of news about its price markup. No day trader could have anticipated this news, and even with stop loss orders, traders who were expecting upward movement in this stock, probably lost more than they expected.

Start Out Slow

As a novice trader, you need to test the waters a bit. Remember, people make and lose money day trading. It's unrealistic for you to expect every move you make to be profitable. This means you should avoid taking on too much risk as well as not risking too much of your investment capital all at once. While testing your trading approach against the market before putting up money is a good idea, keep your initial investments manageable until you gain experience and confidence in your approach. You'll find that things feel different when you actually have money on the line. Beginning day traders should try to understand and manage their reactions to market movements. Make a plan before investing, set entry and departure targets, as well as a target to bail on a stock that's moving in the wrong direction. "My first rule is not to lose money. Losing an opportunity is minor in comparison, because there are always new opportunities around the corner," Burt Dohmen, of Dohmen Capital, said.

Strategies

There are different approaches to investing as a day trader. As you learned earlier in this e-book, you need investments that fluctuate frequently (volatility), and are liquid enough, so you can get in and out of your position quickly and easily.

Once you know what kind of stocks you're going to focus on (if you're focusing on stocks as your investment platform), you need to figure when you're starting a position, and when you're exiting it. As you learned earlier, when you decide to sell, may be even more important than when you decide to buy. There are a number of different strategies a trader can use. We're going to focus on one popular day trading approach. You can learn about others later.

Keep a Journal

Michael Sincere of Market Watch believes day traders should keep a journal of their trades. "Writing down what you did right or wrong will help you improve as a trader," he writes. "... Not surprisingly, you'll probably learn more from your losers than your winners."

Chapter 5:
Intraday Candlestick Pattern

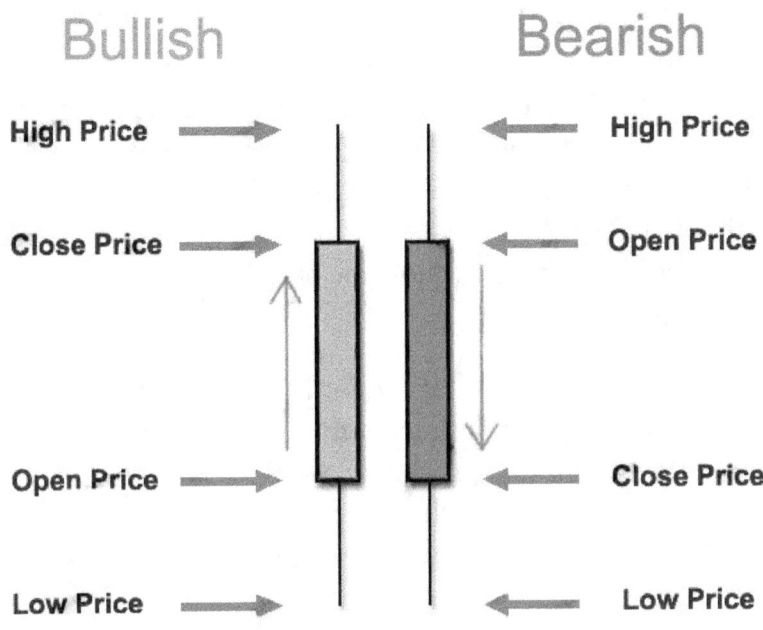

Bullish

High Price ⟶

Close Price ⟶

Open Price ⟶

Low Price ⟶

Bearish

⟵ High Price

⟵ Open Price

⟵ Close Price

⟵ Low Price

"The individual investor should act consistently as an investor and not as a speculator. This means... that he should be able to justify every purchase he makes and each price he pays by impersonal, objective reasoning that satisfies him that he is getting more than his money's worth for his purchase." – Benjamin Graham, author of "The Intelligent Investor."

One method day traders use to analyze stock movements is called a "Candlestick." This tool helps you visualize a stock's movement and try to interpret the meaning of that movement. A candlestick is made up of the share's opening price, closing price, high, and low for a stock over a single day. By following the relationship between candlesticks over a period of time, an investor can get a sense of how other investors are feeling about that stock. Remember, day traders make up a modest number of investors and shares traded in a stock. There are plenty of others investing in a particular stock who have different objectives than you do. A mutual fund may hold a large position in a particular stock as part of its portfolio for a year or longer (funds that are set up to mimic a particular stock index such as the S&P 500, may hold a particular stock for as long as it's followed by that index). The point is movement in a stock's price fluctuates because of the actions of stockholders in general and not because day traders effect price swings.

When using this method, the trader draws one candlestick for each day's trading, and then compares the candlesticks to draw an understanding of the market's views of that stock. Keep in mind, this approach does not give you any indication of why the market views a stock a particular way. In drawing a candlestick, use green for growth and red for decline. Your drawing should look like a candle with a wick at each end. The height of the candle is determined by the amount of distance between the stock's high and low for the day. A tall green candlestick would indicate a strong upward movement; a short one would indicate a much smaller change. The opposite would be true for a red candlestick. The longer the candlestick, the greater the decline that stock has experienced. The "wicks" show the relationship between opening and closing values compared to lows and highs. The bottom wick records the share's opening price (which is why it begins at the bottom of the candle), and extends downward from there. The top wick begins at the closing price (or top of the candle) and extends upward to the stock's high for the day. Learning to read the wicks (sometimes called "shadows") can help you understand more about the stock's movements over time.

Candlestick Pattern -- Bearish

Let's say you've decided on a particular stock. You look at it for the past few days and notice it's followed a rising pattern for three days in a row and then things changed. Suddenly, it's gone from a long green candlestick, to a short green one, followed by a long red one that rises above and below the previous day's candlestick. This "engulfed" look, indicates that investors are becoming more interested in selling the stock than buying it. (A decline in stock price means investors are "bearish" on a stock, while a rise indicates they are "bullish." The terms are used to convey stocks that are sluggish [like a hibernating bear] versus charging [like an angry bull].) The pattern created by this trend is sometimes called "A bearish engulfing pattern."

Candlestick Pattern -- Bullish

Of course stocks can also have a "bullish" pattern. In this case we have a downward trend in our candlesticks. They're red in color, and each day's beginning is lower than the previous day's. If you see a short red candle after several days of downward movements, followed by a longer green candlestick that engulfs the short red candle; you've found a "Bullish engulfing pattern.

Candlestick Pattern – Evening Star Bearish

Sometimes in the candlestick pattern a small red candle will mark the peak of a stock's upward growth. When this happens, the small candle is called a "star". If a long red candle that opens lower than the star's bottom follows the star, the pattern is known as a Bullish Evening Star. The start indicates that stock buyers haven't purchased enough shares to move the stock price past the previous day's high. The long red candlestick that follows can indicate that sellers are replacing buyers.

Candlestick Pattern – Morning Star Bullish

The reverse of the Bearish Evening Star occurs during a downward trend. In this case, a short red candlestick (the "star") is preceded by a long red candlestick. If the star begins lower than the previous candlestick's open, it becomes a stronger indicator. To complete the Bullish Morning Star trend, the start must be followed by a long green candlestick whose open begins higher than the star's open the previous day. If the green candlestick has a short lower wick, you have a stronger indication of the Morning Star. This pattern is interpreted to mean an upward trend in the stock's pricing.

Keep in mind, these are patterns and not cause and effect. As you learned earlier, candlestick patterns offer no insight into why a stock is behaving the way it is. In the stock market it's very possible to have candlesticks indicate one thing, and then have something unexpected (bad news for instance) completely change the stock's direction even though the candlestick pattern contradicts that direction. This is why relying on a pattern system alone without paying attention to other stock indicators can be risky.

Dark Cloud Cover

A Dark Cloud Cover occurs when a bullish (green) candlestick, followed by a bearish (red) candlestick where the closing price ends below the mid point of the previous day's candlestick. If the red candlestick indicates the stock price opened higher than the previous day's close (indicated by the top of the candle being higher than the top of the previous day's handle even though the candle is red), then you have an even stronger indication of a downward trend.

Doji

Sometimes a stock doesn't do anything. Its open and close price doesn't change much, if at all, so the candlestick has no actual body. Instead you see something that has a vertical line and a horizontal line crossing it. A Doji is a neutral sign, but its presence amongst other signs is often important. Many analysts consider a Doji to be an indication of indecision or balance between buyers and sellers. Because they're so close to equal in numbers, there's little to no movement in the stock's price.

A Doji can be an indication of a potential reversal in the stock's price trend, but only if it occurs at a point on the existing "trend" line. (A trend line is a straight line drawn from the minor lows in a rising stock or the minor highs in a declining stock.)

A single Doji becomes less important if it is one of many Doji over a trend line. Not all Doji look alike, and the significance of different Doji shapes can provide you with useful information.

There are several types of Doji. Each one can tell you something about where a stock price may be headed.

- Dragonfly Doji – A Dragonfly Doji shows a very small candle body indicating the open and close are very, very close together (it's not necessary for them to be identical) with a long bottom wick (shadow) protruding from below the candle body. The meaning to this doji is that investors pushed the price of the stock down significantly during the day, but then buyers purchased enough stock to move the stock price back up by the close of the day. This is considered a bullish indicator because it shows there is "support" for the stock's ending price.

- Long Legged Doji ("Rickshaw Man") – The Long Legged Doji shows another very, very small body, but this time both the opening and closing wicks are long. Traders view this as an indication of uncertainty amongst investors.

- Gravestone Doji – This is the opposite of a Dragonfly Doji. While there is still a very, very small candlestick body, it's the upper wick that's quite long and the lower wick that's non-existent. As you'd expect, this is considered a bearish indicator.

Harami

"Harami" are important indicators of potential changes in direction for a stock. The basic Harami is a small candlestick that fits within the previous days candlestick. The Harami's wick shows the opposite direction of the stock's movement. A bearish Harami will have a short red body, with a modest top wick, while a bullish Harami will have a short green body, with a small bottom wick.

A Harami by itself isn't necessary a buy or sell indicator, but if it is followed by a candlestick that followed the Harami's movement, it's a further indication of a trend. A confirmation candlestick is simply a candlestick that continues the trend indicated by the Harami, so a bullish Harami followed by a green candlestick, even a modest one, points to an upward trend. A bearish Harami followed by a red candlestick however modest, can show the opposite.

Sometimes, instead of a Harami candlestick, you'll see a Harami cross. This is simply a Harami made up of a candlestick with a very small body and wicks extending above and below the body. The Harami still needs to be engulfed within the previous day's candlestick. Once again, if the Harami cross follows an upward trend, it is a bearish indicator; while if it follows a downward trend, it is a bullish indicator.

Hammer

Another Candlestick pattern is known as a "Hammer." Hammers are usually considered bullish indicators. They are indicated by a candlestick entry with a small body (either green or red), with a long bottom wick (at least twice the length of the body). Hammers usually occur at the bottoms of downtrend. While both are consider bullish, Hammers where the stock high and its ending price are close (green body candlestick), are considered particularly bullish, while Hammers where the open price and the stock's high are close together, are considered weaker indicators of a downtrend's reversal. It's a good idea to use other indicators to confirm what the Hammer is telling you. Either look for insights in the previous few days' performance, or wait a day to see if the upward movement takes place.

Hanging Man

While the Hanging Man looks very much like a Hammer, the key difference is while the Hammer occurs when the stock is about to reverse a downward trend, while the Hanging Man occurs when a stock has been on an upward trend. Remember, the tail must be at least twice as long as the body. If the tail is longer than this the indication becomes even stronger. It's less important whether the body is green or red, although a red hammer is probably a stronger indication.

The Hammer's long tail is important because it shows that sellers were active. The small body indicates that bullish investors were buying enough stock to keep the price close to its high. If a red candlestick follows a Hammer, the red candlestick is considered a confirmation that a reversal is imminent.

Inverted Hammer

As the name implies, an Inverted Hammer is simply an upside down hammer. What's important is that it manifests near the end of a downtrend. There is a long upper wick with a small (green or red) body at the bottom and no or minimal wick at the top. You need more than an inverted hammer to be sure of a directional change though. Look for other indicators to confirm the reversal such as a green confirmation candle or a break in the trend line.

Shooting Star

This is the opposite of the Inverted Hammer. A Shooting Star presents as a small red or green body with a very long upward wick. The key thing here is that the Shooting Star occurs near the top of an upward trend and can help indicate a period of upward movement in the stock's price is coming to an end. Just like with the Inverted Hammer, a Shooting Star by itself is not enough. You need to look for something to confirm the change in investor mentality.

Chapter 6:
Avoiding Common Mistakes

"Experienced traders control risk, inexperienced traders chase gains." -Alan Farley

It's no secret that being a beginner at anything is tough. A beginner hitter is going to look foolish when facing an experience pitcher, a rookie cornerback will look just as bad against a pro bowl wide receiver, beginning chess players have long suffered the ignominy of the "Fool's Mate," a checkmate that occurs two whole moves into the game.

You can't afford to make these kinds of mistakes since in your case you won't be facing embarrassment, you'll be losing money. Here are some typical beginning trader mistakes and what you can do to avoid them.

- Not having a plan

- Not placing stop loss orders or canceling them unnecessarily

- Staying in a position too long

- Too much leverage

- "Averaging" to make your position more acceptable

- Doing what every one else does

- Trading too aggressively

- Taking on too many markets

- Not doing your homework

- Overconfidence

In this chapter, we'll consider each of these mistakes, and go over why they're so bad for the novice trader.

Not Having a Plan

You've read this at least once already in this book, but it's worth repeating. You need to have a solid plan to succeed at day trading. This plan should include having a trading strategy you understand and are comfortable with, sufficient resources to be able to use the strategy effectively, a buy and sell price and a stop loss price. You should also be knowledgeable about the stock you've picked and the industry it's in.

Not Using Stop Loss Orders or Canceling Them When You Shouldn't

Stop loss orders provide you with at least some protection if your stock choice doesn't work out. You should always set one for every stock you're in. Resist the temptation to cancel a stop loss order just because your investment is nearing the sell point and you feel the stock is going to rebound. This is the action of an emotional trader and not a realistic one.

Staying in a Position Too Long

You're a day trader, not a long-term investor (Well, you can be both, but this e-book is about day trading. You should also maintain separate accounts for long-term holdings). Staying in a position too long risks margin calls. It can also mean your initial analysis missed something. Pull out of the stock and conduct another analysis. Don't just hang in there waiting for something to happen.

Too Much Leverage

While leverage is a powerful investment tool, remember, it magnifies losses as well as gains. Consider what you're willing to risk losing on an investment and limit your risk to that amount and no more. Some gamblers like to "bet big" to cover their losses. Day trading isn't supposed to be gambling. It's supposed to be a systematic effort to make money by investing in the market by taking advantage of short-term movements in prices during the course of a trading day. If you're trying to make a big profit because you need to cover losses, or are looking for an early retirement, your emotion could be clouding your judgment.

Averaging

Long-term investors sometimes employ an investment approach known as "Dollar Cost Averaging." This involves making systematic investments over a prolonged period of time. This tends to smooth out price swings and work in the investors favor over a long period of time provided the stock doesn't travel straight down. The key part of this description are the words "prolonged period of time." DCA as it's known is a smart move for the long-term investor, and if you're also maintaining a long-term investment account, worth considering. It is not a good idea for a day trader though.

The temptation to "average" the cost of a stock lower usually occurs when the stock price is dropping to a point where the investor becomes concerned. Since you are still confident in your analysis, you start to think that if you buy more shares at this new lower price, it will make the average price of a share lower. Then, when the stock price performs as your analysis predicts, you'll make an even greater return. This is another example of emotion overcoming common sense. If the stock price is performing contrary to what your analysis predicted, it is time to end your position and re-evaluate your analysis, not throw more money at a stock that's behaving in an unpredictable manner. "You have to be okay with wins and losses," said Josh Brolin, day trader turned actor. "You can't just be looking for the wins and, when the losses happen, you can't buy more and more because you're sure it's going to bounce. We call that revenge trading."

Doing What Everyone Else Does

Walmart founder Sam Walton had 10 rules for success. Number 10 was "Swim Upstream." In other words don't be afraid to do the opposite of what others are doing. There's actually a whole school of investing called "contrarian investing." You don't have to go that far, but you should understand that if it seems like everybody is focusing on one stock, it might be time to step back and take a closer look at what's going on. In fact this may be time to short that particular stock, especially if you can't see any reason for the stock to be doing what it is. (If you can, then it's likely not a short sale opportunity). Stocks do sometimes become over valued for one reason or another, just as markets do. If you can develop an ability to anticipate corrections, you can make money.

Don't Trade too Aggressively

It can be tempting to enter a lot of positions so you can score big returns. This isn't a good idea for a trader, particularly one who's just starting to day trade. Trying to manage too many trades at one time can cause you to shortchange your research, take too many risks and hurt returns because you're ending up with more losses.

Some traders make only a couple of trades a day, others, with much more experience, may make hundreds. There's no set number of trades you should be aiming at. Of course if you're using a margin account, four trades in five consecutive business days gets you designated as a "pattern" day trader. If you're working through a margin account, you'll be required to maintain a $25,000 minimum in that account or face a margin call. The number of trades you make will not be limited though. If you're using a non-margin account, then you don't have to worry about this requirement.

So how many trades are too many? It depends. (You just knew there was a "just depends" or some other qualification coming didn't you?) How fast can you read? Process information? Locate stocks to trade in? How much money are you comfortable risking at once? One rule of thumb many traders observe is to limit risk to 3% of their portfolios in any one trade. As far as total risk per day? What could you stomach? Are you willing to risk 5%, 10%, 15%, or more? Keep in mind even the best funded, most experienced day traders are fortunate to score a 50% profit on a day's trades. As a beginner, even a 5% return on a day's worth of investments can be overly optimistic.

Taking on Too Many Markets

Since you're new to day trading, trying to take on too many markets is a recipe for loss. It's hard enough to master an understanding of a particular industry, and what drives stock prices in that sector, plus trying to understand its market. Trying to master multiple markets well enough to succeed is just too ambitious.

Not Doing Your Homework

This is how a beginning day trader turns investing into gambling. Going on "instinct," or relying on "tips" from friends or TV "experts," is a recipe for financial ruin. It's fine to consider advice from one of these experts, but only if you research the stock yourself and see how it shapes up based on your trading approach. "The secret to being successful from a trading perspective is to have an indefatigable and an undying and unquenchable thirst for information and knowledge," according to Paul Tudor Jones, founder of Tudor Investment Corporation.

Overconfidence

Overconfidence shouldn't be a problem for a smart beginning day trader. For one thing, you've learned to keep your emotions out of your investing. If you're doing that, then it's unlikely you're over confident. Still, it's worth a warning.

Conclusion

Thank you again for downloading this book!

I hope this book was able to help you to start day trading.

Day Trading is one of the best ways to make money from the comfort of your own home or anywhere you choose- that has an Internet connection. It just requires that you take time to learn the proper strategies upfront and that you don't allow emotional impulses to control your decisions. But if you follow this guide you won't make any of the mistakes that most Day Traders make every day.

The next step is to trade wisely, and continue your investment education.

Finally, if you enjoyed this book, please take the time to share your thoughts and post a review on Amazon. It'd be greatly appreciated!

Thank you and good luck!

www.ingramcontent.com/pod-product-compliance
Lightning Source LLC
Chambersburg PA
CBHW071827200526
45169CB00018B/1157